Tina Tu

The Biography of Tina Turner

Edward Press

TABLE OF CONTENTS

CONCLUSION

INTRODUCTION

From the time she became the lead vocalist of the Ike & Tina Turner Revue in the late '50s, Tina Turner was one of the most explosive soul singers in American music history. Her performances are gritty and growling, harkening back to the early '50s when a combination of gospel passion and free-spirited abandon shaped soul music. After her divorce from Ike in the mid-1970s, she only recorded rarely for the rest of the decade. The mid-'80s saw her comeback as a successful solo artist thanks to a string of hit songs and film roles. As she approached her latter years with a significant impact on younger generations, her fame was sure to last long into the 21st century.

Annie Mae Bullock started singing at age 18. She joined Ike Turner's touring performance as a backup singer. Tina was the center of attention two years later, the highlight of Ike and his Kings of Rhythm's silky-smooth soul extravaganza. Starting with A Fool in Love in 1960, the pair continued to have charting songs throughout the '60s; however, it was difficult to accept the low placement of River Deep, Mountain High, considered one of Phil Spector's most remarkable creations. In 1971, Ike & Tina Turner's Revue reached its pinnacle with the release of Proud Mary, a top-four smash that surpassed everyone's wildest dreams. Behind the scenes, though, Ike became increasingly angry and cruel. In 1976, Tina was able to escape from him for good.

She celebrated her independence by playing Tommy in the film adaptation of Who's rock opera. She had an astonishing, all-too-short performance as the Acid Queen in an otherwise forgettable movie. In the late '70s, she released many albums for United Artists, but her career stopped by the turn of the decade. Surprisingly, Tina made a comeback in 1983, reuniting with a Heaven 17 project called B.E.F. to cover Ball of Confusion, originally by the Temptations. Tina's vocal delivery was predictably apocalyptic, and the following year, she signed a solo contract with Capitol. A rendition of Al Green's Let's Stay Together was her debut song, and it charted in the Top 30 at the beginning of 1984. One of the year's greatest songs, What's Love Got to Do with It, was the album's second single. Private Dancer and Better Be Good to Me were two additional Top Ten songs from the album.

In 1985, she had another film part (Mad Max: Beyond Thunderdome), and its theme song, We Don't Need Another Hero, peaked at number two on the charts. Tina's career peaked with her 1986 smash song, Typical

Male, although she continued to have moderate success with albums such as 1989's Foreign Affair, 1996's Wildest Dreams, and 2000's Twenty-Four Seven. Beyond: Buddhist and Christian Prayers was an album released in 2009 that Turner supervised and to which he added spoken word pieces. The album included vocals by Regula Curti and Dechen Shak-Dagsay. The album was released to the public in 2010. Just in time for Valentine's Day four years later, she released a compilation of her romantic solo songs titled Love Songs.

In 2016, production started on a bio-musical about Turner's life, which she had been working on since the late 2010s. Tina: The Tina Turner Musical, starring Adrienne Warren, premiered in London in 2018. In addition to receiving a Lifetime Achievement Award at that year's Grammys, she also released her second book, Tina Turner: My Love Story.

Tina Turner: Who Was She

During the '50s, Tina Turner joined the musician Ike Turner on stage. After years of marital violence, Tina quit the group in the 1970s, but the Ike and Tina Turner Revue continued to tour and record hits, including Proud Mary, which peaked at number five. Turner's solo career started sluggishly, but she eventually found massive success with her 1984 album Private Dancer. She continued to release top-selling albums and songs, earning her two inductions into the Rock and Roll Hall of Fame. The eight-time Grammy winner subsequently participated in the Religious Beyond project.

CHAPTER 1

<u>Early Years</u>

On November 26, 1939, in Nutbush, Tennessee, Anna Mae Bullock became known as Tina Turner. Anna Mae Bullock and her sister were raised by their grandmother when their destitute sharecropper parents, Floyd and Zelma Bullock, divorced. Anna Mae relocated to St. Louis to live with her mother when her grandmother passed away in the early 1950s.

Anna Mae, a young church choir singer, rapidly became a fixture of the St. Louis R&B scene, where she often frequented Club Manhattan. In 1956, she was a regular customer at the club where she first met rock 'n' roll pioneer Ike Turner, who often performed there with the Kings of Rhythm. She started using the stage name Little Ann and soon became the group's biggest draw.

CHAPTER 2

Professional Career

In 1960, Tina Turner made a huge splash as a lead vocalist on the Rhythm and Blues charts. She had already established herself as a dedicated rock and roll vocalist in her solo career. She has sold over 180 million albums throughout the globe and had 27 singles in the top 10 by the year 2000. What's Love Got to Do with It, a biopic released in 1993, focused on her relationship with Ike Turner. Rolling Stone's top 100 hits of all time included her rendition of River Deep, Mountain High from the 1960s, with the Ike & Tina Turner Review in the top 20 recordings. Even after turning 60, the diva continued to perform to rapt crowds, leaving her legions of followers to wonder at the music that continued after she stopped touring in the year 2000.

Her early musical prowess was evident, but it was during her adolescence in the mid-1950s that she met and eventually married bandleader Ike Turner in St. Louis. Club Manhattan in East St. Louis, Kansas, was the starting point for the partnership. When she initially started performing, Tina Turner went under the moniker Little Anna. However, in 1960, the band's first smash record, A Fool in Love, rocketed to the top of the Rhythm & Blues charts with Tina Turner at the helm as lead vocalist. That record's popularity prompted Ike Turner to reimagine his band as a vehicle for Tina Turner. After that, they began calling themselves the Ike & Tina Turner Review. They went on tour around the country and released many albums and hit songs. The Turners were the Rolling Stones' opening act in the 1960s, and Tina's River Deep, Mountain

High became a crossover success after being recorded by the great Phil Spector.

In the book, I, Tina, co-author Kurt Loder said, "River Deep, Mountain High" was truly a Spector masterpiece. "The music was so unnaturally deep and glossy that it made one feel like they would drown in it. Tina delivered a career-defining performance accompanied by a massive studio orchestra beating out the rumbling chords, a soaring string section, and what seemed like an army of backing vocalists doot-do-dooting along. Some of Spector's earlier music has aged poorly, yet even twenty years later, River Deep can knock your socks off.

Unfortunately, the album flopped. A reclusive Spector. Some have speculated that the single's failure was due to the fact that Spector had already had 26 chart singles in a row before it. Although it only peaked at #88 on the

Billboard Hot 100, River Deep, Mountain High was a massive success in Britain, where it spent 13 weeks at #3. That album never found a good fit, Turner said in her book. It sounded too mainstream on the black stations and too mainstream on the pop ones. Everyone wrote it off. Still, I was pleased with how that album turned out and thought it was something of which to be proud. River Deep revealed to the world what I was capable of.

Let Me Touch Your Mind was Tina Turner's first solo album, released in 1972 during the heyday of the Ike & Tina Turner Review. Her second album, The Country of Tina Turner, was out in 1973. From 1958 through 1978, the Turners dominated the rock and roll scene thanks mainly to the high-energy shows bolstered by the Ikettes, the group's backing vocalists. The Turners' characteristic theme was Proud Mary, a frantic rendition of a well-known standard built from a calm opening to an uncontrollable ruckus of rhythm. The group's version of Proud Mary reached number four on the charts and earned them a Grammy for Best R&B Vocal Performance in 1971.

Damage from Abuse

The public was unaware of the severe domestic violence that afflicted the Turners' marriage throughout their years of fame. Tina Turner, whose husband had been physically and emotionally abusive for a long time, finally snapped in June 1976. Shortly after the couple's first stop in Dallas on their national tour, she was the victim of a brutal assault. Even though the tour was crucial to both of their careers, she gave up on Ike Turner in a moment of despair. She had less than fifty cents in her pocket and didn't tarry to gather her belongings. Tina Turner filed for divorce on

July 27, 1976, and made a tidy sum from the settlement when it was completed in March 1978. Legal fees associated with canceled performances by the Ike & Tina Turner Review were settled with the funds. Tuner handed up the remainder of her money, leaving her with very little. She persisted, though, determined to make a successful career for herself.

By Herself

After graduating from art school in 1977, Turner settled in London, England, and spent the rest of that decade there. The disappointing sales of Turner's 1978 solo album Rough (United Artists) encouraged her to make the decision to engage manager Roger Davies the following year. In 1981, she returned to the States, went on tour with the Rolling Stones, and tried again to revive her career. Three songs from her 1984 album

Private Dancer reached the top 10, including the number one hit What's Love Got to Do with It. She won three Grammys that year for Best Female Pop Vocalist, Best Female Rock Vocalist, and Single of the Year, thanks to this song, which also became her first number-one record. Her 1985 single We Don't Need Another Hero, used in the film Mad Max: Beyond Thunderdome, peaked at number two and earned her widespread acclaim for her remarkable return. In addition, she took home the Grammy for Best Rock Vocal Performance by a Female for her version of One of the Living.

But when she overcame the difficulties of her marriage to Ike Turner, she became weary of justifying the years she had spent under his Svengali influence to the press and the public. To put the affair behind her, she wrote her autobiography, I, Tina, detailing the difficult times in her marriage. The book was out in 1986 and was written in collaboration with rock writer Kurt Loder. In the same year that Back Where You Started won her a Grammy, her album Break Every Rule went multi-platinum. Turner embarked on an 18-month, 25-country global tour in 1987 that continued into 1988. During that time, she gave 220 shows, including a stunning show in Brazil before an audience of 182,000—one of the greatest concert crowds ever. Tina Turner's tours consistently drew sold-out crowds, her albums saw strong sales, and her Tina Live in Europe album for Capitol Records was nominated for a Grammy.

Turner had already been a household name at this point. She rested following the successful tour, and in 1989 she moved back to Europe, purchasing a property in London's Notting Hill Gate neighborhood. After taking a year off, she returned with the mainly self-produced Foreign Affair in 1989.

Film Appearance

Turner had a few appearances in films, but acting was never her primary concern. She played Auntie Entity in Mad Max: Beyond Thunderdome and the Acid Queen in the cinematic adaptation of The Who's rock opera Tommy. Both films were released in 1975. She favored portraying strong female characters.

Rare early footage of the Ike and Tina Turner Review was shown in a British DVD released in 1993 under the title Tina Turner: The Girl from Nutbush. Turner's autobiography, published in 1986, was turned into a film directed by Brian Gibson, which overshadowed the original low-profile endeavor. Kate Lanier wrote the film's script, featuring Angela Bassett and

Laurence Fishburne; Turner kindly offered his services as a creative consultant. Ike Turner avoided endorsing the finished product, and in interviews following the film's release, Turner discussed her wish to move on from the memories shown in it.

Bono, Sheryl Crow, Sting, and Antonio Banderas appeared in Wildest Dreams, which the tireless Turner published in 1996. Turner, approaching 60 at the time, seemed to be a walking dynamo. Twenty-Four Seven, her eighth solo album, was released by Virgin Records in January of 2000 and included collaborations with a number of younger musicians. She released an album for the first time since 1997, which was well received. After all these years, Turner effectively mixes retro-soul with techno flava and is still up to any task, as the Los Angeles Times put it. When her record came out in 2000, she performed at the Super Bowl XXXIV pre-game show and then went on a world tour that started in South Africa and ended at Radio City Music Hall in New York. After 116 performances on her 2000 tour, Turner announced she would be retiring from the road. According to New York Times writer Jon Pareles, Ms. Turner has no plans to retire and become a grand dame who sits back and reflects on her life's successes and failures. She may not win every fight between the sexes, but her voice proves she can hold her own. With ticket sales of $80.2 million, it was the highest-grossing concert tour of 2000.

Many people questioned Turner on her decision to retire when her audience still adored her. After working in the same profession for so long, you start to feel the desire to make a change, Turner told People, adding, I'm still in fantastic condition. I still have the energy. I'm a woman and rock and roll, but you just don't cut it at a certain age. She still intended to release new albums and perform live sometimes.

Story of a Private Dancer's

Turner's followers are surprised to learn that her wild antics and yelling during performances are all part of the act. She's far more little and subdued in person than she seems on stage or in her songs. EbonyHedda .'s Maye and Robyn Foyster dubbed her the embodiment of traditional elegance with a timeless sense of taste. After splitting up with Ike Turner in 1977, she relocated to London; from there, she went to Cologne, Germany; and finally, in 1998, she settled in Zurich, Switzerland, where she bought a mansion she lived with Erwin Bach, a German record label executive she had been dating since 1986. Turner has said several times that she and Bach have no intention of getting married. She told United Press International, We're like an old married couple already, so we don't see the necessity. Anna Fleur, her custom-built home near Cap Ferrat, France, is another of her favorite places to stay. She gushed to Swiss News that "it affords me security" to be based in Europe. It's where I've had the most success and felt the most valued.

She is the proud matriarch of her family, having raised sons Craig and Ron and now her grandchildren and great-grandchildren. She began studying Buddhism not long before she split from Ike Turner, and she remains a devout follower. It has been said that Turner is a homebody who takes pleasure in interior design and Bach's home cooking.

Turner's success on the charts has persisted even after he retired. All the Best, a greatest hits album released in 2005, arrived at number two on the charts. The album included three brand new tracks, one of which, Open Arms, topped the Adult Contemporary radio charts only four weeks after its release, giving the diva yet another smash success. Fred Bronson of Billboard speculated that All the Best might mark a new era in Turner's lengthy career.

CHAPTER 3

<u>Career Highlight</u>

Tina Turner often frequented St. Louis's nightlife establishments. Her future husband, Ike Turner, and his band, the Kings of Rhythm, were performing at Club Manhattan, where she met them. Ike saw her potential and offered her the opportunity to sing in his 1958 recordings.

The duo of Tina Turner and Ike released their first song together, A Fool in Love, in 1960, which peaked at #2 on the Hot R&B Sides chart. A Grammy Award nomination followed the release of It's Gonna Work Out Fine.

In 1964, the pair signed with Warner Bros. Records subsidiary label Loma Records due to their rising popularity. They toured the country performing live and appeared on programs like Hollywood A Go-Go.

She released her first single, River Deep - Mountain High, on Philles Records in 1966. As a result of the song's success in the UK, Turner was invited to serve as the tour's opening act for The Rolling Stones.

She released the albums Come Together and Workin' Together with Ike after signing with Liberty Records in 1970. Turner and Ike's rising national profile led to an invitation to appear on The Ed Sullivan Show.

With the support of Bolic Sound Studios, Turner recorded her first solo album Tina Turns the Country On!, in 1974. The album earned her praise from critics and a Best Female R&B Vocal Performance Grammy nomination.

Ike and Turner have continued their musical collaboration. After that, they made an album called The Gospel According to Ike & Tina, in which they attempted gospel music. They were up for Best Soul Gospel Performance, and it was an immediate smash.

Tina Turner portrayed The Acid Queen in the London musical Tommy 1974. The following year, she released her second solo album, The Acid Queen, which cemented her status as a household name in the U.K. thanks to her performance.

With the support of United Artists Records, Turner gave cabaret-style performances in Las Vegas in 1978 in an attempt to revive her career. She has had guest appearances on television programs, such as The Hollywood Squares and Donny and Marie.

The same record company issued her third album, Rough, in 1978. Then Love Explosion came out. She opted not to extend her contract with the label since her albums had failed to connect with her audience.

Turner was featured in New York's The Ritz in 1980 after she had begun working with Roger Davies. Because of this, she was able to share the stage with Rod Stewart on S.N.L. and later on his U.S. tour.

Tina Turner's Let's Stay Together was released in 1983, shortly after she had signed with Capitol Records. The song became a worldwide phenomenon. The record label gave her a three-album contract.

Private Dancer, released in 1984, is widely regarded as her comeback album. About 20 million copies of the record were sold throughout the globe. She won a Grammy for the smash song What's Love Got to Do with It? from her album of the same name.

Turner's 1985 appearance in Mad Max Beyond Thunderdome followed the success of her record. The film was a smash hit, and her performance earned her the NAACP Image Award for Outstanding Actress.

Her second platinum-selling album, Break Every Rule, was published in 1986. Her star on the Hollywood Walk of Fame was unveiled the same year as the publication of her autobiography, I, Tina.

In 1988, she made headlines when she and Paul McCartney performed in Rio de Janeiro's Maracana Stadium in front of the world's biggest-paying crowd. The feat was documented and entered into the record books.

In 1995, she collaborated with U2 to write a song for the James Bond film Golden Eye. Success with it led to the release of Wildest Dreams, which was certified gold in the United States and platinum in Europe.

During the 2005 Kennedy Center Honors, Turner was recognized for her work, and many famous people, such as Oprah Winfrey, Melissa Etheridge, Queen Latifah, Beyonce, and Al Green, paid homage to her. Even George W. Bush, the president, thought she was great.

She received a Grammy for River: The Joni Letters in 2008 and performed at the ceremony alongside Beyonce. In the same year, she went on her Tina!: 50th Anniversary Tour, her first concert tour in 10 years.

In 2018, she launched TINA: The Tina Turner Musical, a jukebox musical that summarizes her life. Phyllida Lloyd and Stage Entertainment worked together to publish it. Adrienne Warren starred in the production's debut in London. Tina Turner: My Love Story, her second autobiography, was published the same year.

In 2012, Tina Turner was in Beijing for the Giorgio Armani fashion presentation. She made history when, the following year, she graced the cover of the German edition of Vogue as the magazine's oldest cover model.

CHAPTER 4

Key Productions

Turner's career took off with the publication of her fifth album, 1984's Private Dancer. It helped her succeed when she really needed it, just after her divorce severely damaged her career.

For her album Private Dancer, Tina Turner won four Grammys. What's Love Got to Do with It, the album's breakout tune, became her anthem. The album topped the charts all around the globe, including the U.S.A.

CHAPTER 5

<u>Honors and Awards</u>

Turner's breakout album, Private Dancer, garnered four of her twelve Grammy Awards. The year's number-one song was What's Love Got to Do with It, which won many prizes. For the music of Mad Max: Beyond Thunderdome, she took home yet another Grammy. Grammys have also been presented for her albums Back Where You Started From, Tina Live in Europe, and River: The Joni Letters.

The Rock & Roll Hall of Fame has inducted Turner. Three of her albums are in the Grammy Hall of Fame: River Deep - Mountain High, Proud Mary, and What's Love Got to Do with It. She won the Grammy for Lifetime Achievement this year (2018).

CHAPTER 6

Personal life

Tina had a connection with the Kings of Rhythm saxophonist Raymond Hill in the late '50s. She was a senior in high school at the time. During her final year of high school, Tina fell pregnant with Raymond. Craig was born to Tina and Hill in 1958, although the couple had already broken up at that time.

Ike Turner, Tina's musical collaborator since 1962, is her husband. Two years ago, they had a boy, and they named him Ronnie. They co-parented Ike's two boys from a previous relationship with Ronnie and Craig. Tina and Ike's divorce was formalized on March 29, 1978, with the couple citing irreconcilable differences as the reason. Ronnie died in December of 2022 from colon cancer.

In 1986, Tina crossed paths with German music executive Erwin Bach. Erwin is 16 years younger than her. In 1995, Tina and Erwin uprooted to Switzerland. Tina, in particular, had always admired the cleanliness and stability of Swiss society. Since they were not citizens, they rented a huge home on the shores of Lake Zurich for the next twenty or so years. After 27 years of dating, they tied the knot at their house in July 2013.

Tina filed for Swiss citizenship in the new year of 2013. She took and passed all necessary exams and in April 2013, was given Swiss citizenship. In October 2013, she renounced her citizenship to the United States.

CHAPTER 7

<u>Tina Turner Networth</u>

At the time of her death, Tina Turner, a singer, and songwriter, was worth $250 million. Tina Turner has sold more albums than almost anybody else. She sold over 200 million albums globally over her career. Her strong singing voice and extended professional life made her famous. She was honored with a total of 12 Grammys, three of which were for Hall of Fame status. Tina stopped performing permanently in 2009. In October of 2021, Tina, who has earned the title Queen of Rock and Roll, was inducted into the Rock and Roll Hall of Fame.

Since the mid-1990s, Tina has called Switzerland home. As of April 2013, she is a citizen of Switzerland. She gave up her U.S. citizenship in October 2013.

Tina received $50 million from B.M.G. Rights Management for her songs, likeness, and image rights in 2021.

CONCLUSION

Turner had some serious health problems in her 70s. Turner had a stroke in 2013, only three months after her wedding to Bach. She was told she had colon cancer in 2016. She received a new kidney the following year from a donor which was Bach.

To kick out 2018, an exciting year for the 78-year-old Turner, she was recognized with a Grammy Lifetime Achievement Award (together with other industry icons like Neil Diamond and Emmylou Harris).

In March of that year, Turner said she had long forgiven her ex-husband for the abuse he had committed against her. She told The Times of London, As an older person, I have forgiven him, but it would not work with him. I emphatically declined in response to his request for a last trip with me. You couldn't just let Ike back in after forgiving him.

The launch of TINA: The Tina Turner Musical at London's Aldwych Theatre in April gave fans a chance to see her most famous songs performed onstage. The following autumn, it debuted at New York's Broadway theater.

Turner's eldest son, Craig, was discovered shot to death in his Studio City, California, home in the summer of 2018. The age of the realtor was 59. In her second book, My Love Story, released in October, she discussed his death and other topics.

Turner was inducted into the Rock and Roll Hall of Fame for the second time in October 2021, three years later, but this time as an individual. Tina, an HBO biopic, premiered at the beginning of the year and contained archive material as well as interviews with

Turner, Angela Bassett, Oprah Winfrey, and others. The Tina Turner Barbie doll was also released that year as a tribute.

Ronnie Turner, Turner's son, passed away at age 62 in 2022 due to colon cancer and cardiovascular illness. Turner lamented Ronnie's untimely passing on Instagram: Ronnie, you departed the earth way too early. When I shut my eyes in grief, I think of you, my dear son.

Printed in Great Britain
by Amazon

22963349R00030